The Parable of
the Talents

Text and illustrations copyright © Daniel Collins 1995

Published by
Barnabas
an imprint of
The Bible Reading Fellowship
Peter's Way
Sandy Lane West
Oxford
OX4 5HG
ISBN 0 7459 3246 0
Albatross Books Pty Ltd
PO Box 320
Sutherland
NSW 2232
Australia
ISBN 0 7324 0935 7

First edition 1995
10 9 8 7 6 5 4 3 2 1 0

A catalogue record for this book is available
from the British Library

Barnabas ™ is a trademark of The Bible Reading Fellowship

Printed and bound in Hong Kong

The Parable of the Talents

Jesus told this story:
Once there was a man
who was about to go
on a journey.

He called his servants and put them in charge of his property, giving to each one according to his ability.

I will give you 5,000 gold coins

To another servant he gave 2,000 gold coins...

The first servant went at once and invested his money—perhaps he bred sheep—and earned another 5,000 gold coins.

In the same way the second servant earned another 2,000 coins— perhaps he grew corn.

But the third servant went off, dug a hole in the ground, and hid his master's money.

After a long time the master came back and he called his servants in order to see how they had used his money.

The servant who had received 5,000 coins handed over the other 5,000 that he had earned.

Well done, you good and faithful servant! I will put you in charge of large amounts!

Then the servant who had received 2,000 coins handed over the other 2,000 that he had earned.

Well done, good and faithful servant! Come on in and share my happiness!

Then the servant who had received 1,000 coins said...
I know you are a hard man... I was afraid, so I hid your money in the ground.
The master was very angry. He took the 1,000 gold coins from the servant and threw him out of the house.

And he gave the 1,000 gold coins to the servant who had 10,000.

To every person who has something, even more will be given . . . but the person who has nothing, even the little that he has will be taken away from him.